5

D1572113

Shaftesbury

Bell Street   J. R. BIGGS

SHAFTESBURY

The 'Shaston' of
THOMAS HARDY

Including fourteen wood engravings
with a memoir of James Masters
and the High House Press
by John R. Biggs

SHAFTESBURY
AT THE BOOK IN HAND
1983

© Copyright : Christopher Driver and John R. Biggs

Published by the Book in Hand, Bell Street, Shaftesbury
1983

ISBN 0 9508868 0 7

Printed and bound by Butler & Tanner Limited
Frome and London.

INTRODUCTION

It is just over fifty years since the original edition of this book, now long out of print, was produced in the town it portrays; and forty years since the death of its author, designer and printer, James Masters. The present facsimile is issued from a nearby address, as a tribute to Masters and his High House Press, and as an opportunity for a new generation of Shastonians to acquire a distinguished series of engravings, depicting a Shaftesbury that for the most part, happily, remains intact.

All the High House Press books and booklets are now collectors' pieces, hard to find and expensive to buy. The bibliography at the end of the book lists forty-four titles produced under the imprint between 1924 and 1936, while James and Beatrice Masters lived in Shaftesbury High Street. The scrupulous elegance of their books earned for them a place among the best private printing of the period at exhibitions in London and San Francisco.

By fortunate circumstance it has been possible to have a new foreword written especially for this edition by John R. Biggs, who cut eight of the wood engravings for the original edition at the time, just after leaving college, when he was living and working with James and Beatrice Masters at the High House. The frontispiece to this present edition, looking back along Bell Street from the junction with Angel Lane, was also cut by him, but omitted from the original. John Biggs,

Master of the Art Workers Guild for 1983, has recently lectured on design education in Chicago, Hong Kong, Tokyo and the Soviet Union. He lives in Brighton, and now tells his own story about a couple whom others in Shaftesbury also remember, down to the "necklace of beads as big as bed-knobs" that Beatrice Masters often wore in her gift shop.

SHAFTESBURY   Walter J. Partridge
1983   Christopher Driver

My connections with James Masters and the High House Press
by John R. Biggs

I first got to know James and Beatrice Masters in 1930 or 1931, while I was still a student at the Derby School of Art. Encouraged by A. J. A. Symons of the First Edition Club, I had become enthusiastic about wood-engraving and book production.

There were two evening newspapers in Derby at that time, the *Telegraph* and the *Express*. The *Telegraph* was offering its readers free life insurance and other inducements in an attempt to destroy its competitor. The *Express* succumbed to the attack and all its printing plant was put up for sale. I went to see the works manager, who sympathised with an impecunious teenager and let me have an Albion press for thirty shillings, a composing frame for one shilling, type cases threepence each, one or two chases and a composing stick. I was so excited, I hired a hawker's barrow from the nearby market and hauled the Albion home through the busy Saturday evening crowds in the centre of Derby. So I became hooked on printing and began writing round for a job in publishing when I finished at the Art School. I was advised, wisely as it turned out, to complete the course first and obtain the Art Teachers'

Diploma which would serve me for the rest of my life.

My first contact with James Masters was, I believe, the result of this writing around. There followed a fruitful friendship that lasted until he moved to Westbury-on-Trym in 1936. By that time I was married, living and working in London, and our correspondence gradually dwindled to extinction.

James and Beatrice Masters were a devoted couple. They invited me to stay with them at their High House, which was a gift or souvenir shop in Shaftesbury High Street, at the foot of Muston's Lane. The room over the shop, facing the High Street, was the dining room and printery, with their Albion press in a corner by the window. It seemed quite natural to be eating beside the press with proofs lying around. James, who I believe had been a teacher (though he sometimes spoke of the uselessness of schools), was dedicated to printing. He had an innate good taste in typography, and was prepared to work well into the night to get the press-work right. Of the dozen or so letters that I still possess, most of them say that he has been working late and is tired. One says that he was working till 3 a.m. and will be glad when the job is finished.

Apart from his enthusiasm for private press books, he was what we now might call a music buff. He loved to retire to the back sitting room, which had a marvellous view over the Blackmore Vale, and put records of classical music on a gramophone with fibre needles—the triangular sort by E. M. Ginn, which required cutting from time to time. I knew virtually nothing about music and James loved to be avuncular and introduce me to his favourite records of Brahms and Beethoven.

I well remember his delight at the revelation it was to me when I first heard Scarlatti played by Wanda Landowska on the harpsichord. It opened my eyes, or rather my ears, to the beauty of the harpsichord. Music and Masters were, to me, inseparable.

But it was typography and printing in which he excelled as a practitioner, and he was highly respected by some of the best printers and critics of book production. He had a friendly relationship with Bernard Newdigate, who wrote about book production in the London Mercury. My engraving of the interior of Old Grove's Place, which is reproduced in this book, was printed in the London Mercury with encouraging comments.

The distinguished typophile Beatrice Warde (Paul Beaujon) visited James at Shaftesbury and occasionally stayed the weekend. On one occasion James took me to Douglas Cleverdon's book shop in Bristol, where at the back of the shop he had a press on which he had produced "The Ancient Mariner", illustrated by David Jones. I took a photograph of the fascia board above the shop window, which had been painted by Eric Gill in sans serif letters. This is the only photograph known to have been taken of this origin of one of Gill's famous types. Later the full alphabet was designed, in capitals only, eventually to be completed and sold as Gill Sans.

Masters liked to talk about typography and seemed pleased to have a youngster around who was as enthusiastic as he was about hand-made paper, good presswork, letter and word spacing, appropriate margins, patterned cover papers and, most of all, the choice of type faces. He had a fount of type called Cloister (based on the Jenson face), including a twelve-point titling, which gave a wide variety of typographic tones of voice in the one body size. As I had no type at all, he gave me the Cloister in payment for the engraving I did (in 1932) for the original first issue of this " Shaftesbury " book, and treated himself to some founts of Bembo type which he was beginning to favour (who wouldn't?).

I used the Cloister to produce a slim volume of my own youthful poems, " Sinfin Songs ". Three copies of this I bound in leather in Douglas Cockerell's book-binding class at the Central School of Art and Crafts in London. I also cut the tools for decorating the cover, and through the First Edition Club, three copies were exhibited in the Golden Gate Exhibition in San Francisco.

Masters had done a little etching but no wood-engraving. As the engravings for the drawings I had done in Shaftesbury developed, he became keen to try engraving himself, and asked me to show him the techniques. He learned quickly and soon produced a number of very proficient blocks which are included with my own in this book.

While I was staying with them in Shaftesbury, James and Beatrice took me to meet William J. Ibbett, the poet, who lived nearby. Ibbett's " Facets of Winter and Spring ", including a preface by Paul Beaujon, was printed by Masters in 1931, with a few decorations which I had engraved. I made a sketch of Ibbett which I hope to engrave sometime; but one thing he said which I have never forgotten. It was about writing poetry. He said, " Create in haste, correct at leisure ". I knew what he meant.

Looking back, I think I owe a lot to James and Beatrice

Masters. They appeared to live and work in harmony in a way few couples enjoy. He was the first artist–craftsman in print that I had met and he was an example and an inspiration. In later life it is always difficult to be sure where one's ideas came from, but I believe some of the threads of thought were woven into the fabric of my mind by the experience of working with James and Beatrice at the High House.

John R. Biggs
1983

SHAFTESBURY: the *Shaston* of Thomas Hardy

TWELVE WOOD ENGRAVINGS
BY JOHN R. BIGGS AND
JAMES E. MASTERS

SHAFTESBURY
AT THE HIGH HOUSE PRESS
1932

The Contents

¶ *The engraving of* HIGH HOUSE
on title-page is by John R. Biggs.

Foreword

THIS LITTLE BOOK is not a guide to, nor a history of Shaftesbury: its purpose is an endeavour to record some picturesque spots and corners as they appear to-day—or perhaps, by the time the book is published, as they were yesterday! Changes are swift, and one of the illustrations already represents a thing of the past. The note opposite the engraving of *Haimes Lane* explains that one of the thatched roofs had gone, but since the note was printed one of the remaining cottages has been re-roofed with slate, and what was a picturesque group of cottages is gradually degenerating into just an ordinary street corner. Though modern "improvements" seem bound to creep into even so tiny a town, Shaftesbury has not yet been altogether spoilt. During recent years some of the thatched roofs have given place to tiles and slates, and in a few cases to what is worse—corrugated iron. New houses and cottages of brick are springing up, and some of the old shops are glorified with modern fronts, but many thatched cottages and quaint corners remain; and the vast expanse of surrounding country visible from the heights of Shaftesbury still retains its natural and rustic charms.

" Shaston, the ancient British Palladour . . . . was, and is, in itself the city of a dream." Thus Thomas Hardy describes it in *Jude the Obscure,* and so it is even to-day, despite encroachments by the modern builder. Situated in the north-eastern corner of the county of Dorset and perched on the summit of an almoſt perpendicular hill seven hundred feet above the sea level, Shaftesbury occupies a unique position commanding glorious and almoſt illimitable views of an unbroken succession of green fields and undulating hills and valleys. " This breezy and whimsical spot" is the scene of aɛtion in Part IV ("At Shaſton") of *Jude the Obscure,* and there Hardy gives one of the fineſt descriptions of Shaftesbury ever penned. The school where Phillotson and Sue taught, and the "ancient dwelling across the way" where they lived, ſtill exiſt and may easily be found and recognised from Hardy's description of them.

In the case of *Shaſton,* Hardy did not, as was his wont, invent or use a fiɛtitious placename: he simply retained an old one. The mileſtones all round ſtill record the diſtances to *Shaſton,* and the name is often used by the inhabitants to this day.

The earlieſt name of Shaftesbury was *Caer Palladour,* the town of the shaft or tower; probably from one of the round towers which the early inhabitants of Britain were accuſtomed to ereɛt on lofty eminences. According to tradition, such a tower or caſtle once ſtood on Caſtlè Hill, where traces of ancient masonry and earthworks have been found. The name may also have been derived from the temple to Pallas which is said to have exiſted in Shaftesbury at the time of the occupation of Britain by the Romans. The position of the temple is not known, but the Rev. J. J. Reynolds, in his *Ancient Hiſtory of Shaftesbury,* surmises that it may have been on the present site of High House, where " Roman Architeɛtural remains . . . . seemingly of a building of considerable magnitude and importance were discovered."

Shaftesbury is one of the oldest, and also one of the smallest towns in England. According to Geoffrey of Monmouth, it was built by Hudibras, King of Britain, in 950 B.C., but its real history begins with the foundation of the Abbey by Alfred the Great in 880 A.D. The Abbey was rased to the ground after the Dissolution in 1539, and few traces of it remain. Excavations were made on the site in 1861-2 and were later re-opened and extended by Mr. E. Doran Webb, F.S.A. Further excavations were carried out under the direction of Mr. J. Wilson Claridge in 1931, when, amongst many relics and objects of interest, a leaden casket containing remains conjectured to be those of King Edward the Martyr was found. Edward was murdered by his stepmother, Elfrida, at Corfe Castle in 978 and buried at Wareham, but three years later his remains were translated to the Royal Abbey of Shaftesbury, which then became a place of pilgrimage.

King Canute died at Shaftesbury in November 1035, but his remains were removed to Winchester for burial.

Shaftesbury at one time possessed twelve churches and three mints, but the mints have vanished, and of the four remaining churches one only, St. Peter's, is of ancient date. From its tower the curfew is still rung every night.

Gone are the mediæval glories of the ancient hill-town, but the Shaftesbury of to-day is a pleasant place, and its commanding position and scenic beauty make it one of the most delightful spots in all England.

J. E. M.

SHAFTESBURY
November 1932

SHAFTESBURY is best seen from the south, with its cottages straggling up the hill to the two churches of Holy Trinity and St. Peter's at the top.

Shaftesbury

J. R. BIGGS

STANDING in the High Street, where its northern wall sinks right into the pavement, is the church of St. Peter's, an early fifteenth-century building in the Perpendicular style. The church has a noble tower, and the wall of the north aisle is surmounted by a fine battlemented parapet rich with carvings of roses, portcullises & pomegranates; but the interior, except for some beautiful vaulting in the roof of the western porch, is bare and disappointing. On all sides but the North the church is hemmed in by buildings; and this view from the South shows only the tower and the western porch. The house seen on the right was formerly the *Sun and Moon* Inn, the cellars of which ran under the church.

St. Peter's Church   J. R. BIGGS

EXCEPT for a few modern shop-fronts and one very ugly erection in the centre of the town, the High Street of Shaftesbury remains much as it was when Thomas Hardy wrote *Jude the Obscure*. Here is an unusual view which has the advantage of missing the modern "improvements" in the street.

High Street   J. R. BIGGS

C

GOLD HILL is a ſteep and ancient cobbled ſtreet bounded on one side by a massive buttressed wall which encloses and supports what was, centuries ago, the Abbey garden. At the top of the hill ſtand St. Peter's church and the Town Hall, the back of which is here seen. *Goldhulle* is mentioned as far back as 1352 in a deed of that date preserved in the Town Hall, and the name was probably derived from one of the three mints which once exiſted in Shaftesbury.

Gold Hill   J. E. MASTERS

SEEN from the top, Gold Hill presents a picturesque view of tiled and thatched cottages and
massive age-worn buttresses of greenish-gray
stone set against a distant background of undulating
hills and fields; all uniting to make what Thomas
Hardy, in *Jude the Obscure*, calls "one of the queerest
and quaintest spots in England."

Gold Hill   J. R. BIGGS

D

COPPICE STREET was, until a few years ago, a pretty country lane with a small coppice at the end furthest from the town, but the hedges and fields have now vanished from one side of the lane and given place to rows of new and uninteresting brick houses. At the end of the street leading into the town, however, are many old stone-built and thatched cottages unspoilt by the modern builder. *Coppestrete* is mentioned as early as 1388 in a deed dated "Thursday before S. Barnabas Day, 11 Richard II." Five years later it was *Copstret*, and on a map dated 1615 it is *Copstreet Lane.*

Coppice Street

J. E. MASTERS

HERE is, or was, a picturesque little group of thatched cottages. Since this engraving was made, the nearest cottage has been rebuilt and its thatched roof replaced, alas, with one of corrugated iron! Such is modern progress.

Haimes Lane   J. R. BIGGS

E

PHILLOTSON'S school in *Jude the Obscure* is the Shaftesbury Infants School. Here it was that Jude met Sue on his visit to Shaſton.

The School Playground   J. R. BIGGS

"THAT ancient dwelling across the way called Old-Grove's Place" will be remembered by readers of *Jude the Obscure* as the abode of Phillotson and Sue. The house, " whose walls were lined with wainscoting of panelled oak reaching from floor to ceiling," remains as Thomas Hardy describes it; and the clothes-closet where one night Sue hid herself, and the window from which she jumped may still be seen. Standing in the street called Bimport, the house, with its projecting porch and iron-studded door, is easily recognised. Inside the porch is another and very massive iron-studded oak door which has a curious warped appearance. This quaint old door folds back in the centre, as may be seen in the wood-engraving, a view looking from the interior towards the entrance-porch.

Interior, Old Grove's Place   J. R. BIGGS

F

THE PARK WALK is a delightful tree-lined terrace situated on the very edge of the hill on which Shaftesbury stands. On the south is an extensive view unsurpassed by few in England, and on the north side a wall encloses the site of the Abbey excavations. At the foot of the hill lies the parish of St. James with its many varied roofs and its church tower prominent in the landscape.

St. James from the Park Walk   J. E. MASTERS

BELOW the Park Walk is Laundry Lane, where once stood the laundry belonging to the Abbey of Shaftesbury.

Laundry Lane

J. E. MASTERS

THIS quaint old stone pump is still in use as the source of water supply to the dwellers in Andrews Yard, a little square sheltered under the hill and enclosed on three sides by cottages, and on the fourth by a low stone wall and railings in the main street of St. James.

Andrews Yard   J. E. MASTERS

Printed and made in England by
JAMES E. MASTERS
THE HIGH HOUSE PRESS
SHAFTESBURY DORSET
November, 1932

High House Press Book List

1924 Twenty Four Sonnets of William Joseph Ibbett. 29pp (165).
—— The Eve of Venus by W. J. Ibbett. 16pp (115).
—— Rocky Valley and Other Poems by N. C. Raad. 24pp (250).
1925 A Greek Garland of Amorous Trifles trs. W. J. Ibbett. 25pp (140).
—— A Ballade Upon a Wedding by Sir John Suckling. 15pp (150).
—— The Shepheard's Holy Day. 11pp (170).
—— Young Folk and Old by Eleanor Farjeon. 23pp (220).
—— Poems by Lewis W. Townsend. 21pp (158).
—— Twilight Corners by D. G. Hutton. (165).
1926 Songs of Petrarch trs W. J. Ibbett. 30pp (105).
—— The Gossips, 15th century poem. (100).
—— Mildred, 12 essays by various hands. (112).
—— Twenty Songs of William Shenstone. (192).
—— Songs and Verses from Edmund Waller. 24pp (150).
1927 Rymes of the Minstrels. 32pp (230).
—— The Vigil of Venus trs by Thomas Parnell. 12pp (200).
—— The Room and Other Poems by Eric Walter White. 24pp (180). (The first book which Mrs. Masters helped set).
—— The First Three Odes of Anacreon trs. by Ambrose Phillips. 10pp (100).
1928 A Pastoral Ballad by William Shenstone. 16pp (120).
—— The Harmony of Birds, attributed to John Skelton, printer John Wight, c. 1555 32pp (160).
—— The Reckoning and other poems by E. M. Martin. 27pp (150).
—— Good Wine a fifteenth century drinking song. (90).
1929 Hylas the XIIIth Idyll of Theokritos, trs. S. Matthewman. 8pp (200).
—— Twenty-six Sonnets of Petrarch trs. W. J. Ibbett. 30pp (165).
—— An Anatomie of the World by John Donne. 32pp (170).
1930 Twelve Songs From the Plays of John Lyly. 18pp (160).
—— Arcades by John Milton. 8pp (100).
—— The Poem of Amriolkais trs. Sir William Jones. 27pp (200).
—— The High House Press, a short history by S. Matthewman. 8pp (500).

1931 A Medley, some verses by William J. Ibbett. 15pp (155).

—— One Hundred Facets of Winter and Spring by W. J. Ibbett. 38pp plus 4pp intro (loose) by Paul Beaujon (Beatrice Warde). With wood engravings by J. R. Biggs and John Masters.

1932 Shaftesbury: The Shaston of Thomas Hardy by J. R. Masters. viiipp + 24 leaves printed one side only. A signed limited edition on h.m. paper and an unlimited edition on Basingwerk parchment.

—— Goethe, Faust trs. Shelley.

1933 Pannychis by Eleanor Farjeon. 14pp (225).

—— Christmas by George Wither. (50).

—— How a Merchant Did Betray His Wife, a 15th cent. ballad. 23pp (100).

1935 Horace 365 short quotations from, trs. H. Darnley Naylor. vii + 92pp (215).

1936 A Marriage Triumphe by Thomas Heywood. 31pp (65). The first book issued after the move to Westbury-on-Trym.

—— Hero and Leander trs. by George Chapman. (75).

1937 Romany Joter by Dorothy Una Ratcliffe. 16pp (115).

—— Six Poems by N. L. Bright.

—— Old English Wines and Cordials compiled by J. E. Masters wood engravings by Reynolds Stone.

nd The Art of Making Fine Prints.

1939 Patient Grizelda.

—— This Greeting With Our Good Wishes for the New Year 1939. Signed wood engraving by James E. Masters. 4pp. (There were many other Christmas greetings printed by Masters at the High House Press).

Note: pp = number of pages
(115) = number of copies printed, where known.
trs. = translated by
nd = not dated.

W.J.P.
1983